ENGLISH IS FUN

LEARN ENGLISH

SANVI

I dedicated this book to make sure that everybody learn and speak English in a very nice way . Actually , English is so simple as your mother tongue . I would prefer everybody to use this book .

Contents

Preface

Communication is the essence of human experience and in order to communicate meaningfully , we shoul possess the necessary language skills . It is natural to start by speaking what we hear areound us . With the passage of time , we gradually and unconscioulу evelop a better understanding of correctly using our mother tongue . But when we learn a new language , such as English , we should endeavour to make sure that accuracy underpins all our communication in it . So it becomes imperative that we study the grammar of the English language to be able to communicate better in the language .

Author

CHAPTER ONE

SOME BASIC TERMS OF ENGLISH

Get set go...

a . is / am / are

We use is/am/are to tell something which is a habit .

IS

Used with he , she , it and any name

AM

Used only with I

ARE

Used with we, you , they and names more than 1

Let's perfect it

Q1 . Write any 3 sentences with "is" that you use in your daily life .

1

2

3

Q2 .Write any 3 sentences with "am" that you use in your daily life

1

2

3

Q3 Write any 3 sentences with "are" that you use in your daily life

1

2

3

B . Has / have

It shows ownership of something

Has

Used with he ,she , it and any one name

For ex:

Rahul has a book .

She has a beautiful frock .

Have

Used with we , you , they and I

For ex:

We have books.

I have a magnet .

Let's perfect it

Write 2 sentences with has and have which you use in your daily .

3. was/were

It shows what had happened . Was and were are in the past tense.

Was

Used with I , He , she , it and any name

For ex :

I was playing .

She was going .

Were

Used with We, You . They and names more than one .

For ex-

They were not studying.

We were playing with our dolls .

Let's perfect it

A . Write two sentences on "was" that you use in daily life .

1 . 2 .

B . Write two sentences on "were" that you use in daily life .

1 . 2 .

CHAPTER TWO

Subject and Predicate

Subject

Who or what the sentence is about .

For ex

The alligator eats cookies .

Who ?

The alligator

So, "the alligator " is the subject .

Predicate

What the subject is,has or does

For ex

The alligator eats cookies .

What do it do ?

eats cookies .

So eats cookies is the predicate

Let’s look at other examples

Lily is a beautiful flower .

What is beautiful flower?

Lily

So lily is subject

What is lily ?

is a beautiful flower .

Note-a subject may be single or it may contain group of words.

for ex

1 . Rajni ate an apple.

subject - Rajni

2 . The beautiful peacocks danced in the rain .

subject - The beautiful peacocks

exercise -

Q1 . Underline the subject .

1 . Rohit and his parents went to the zoo.

2 . Jay and his dog run on the beach every meaning .

3 . The boys are playing cricket .

4 . She is reading a book .

Q2 . Find the predicate

1 . The clever magician amazed the children with his superb tricks .

2 . The mouse ate the cheese and ran away .

3 . Vedika opened an umbrella .

CHAPTER THREE

Article

What are articles ?

Articles are a kind of adjectives that describe noun .
For ex

1 . The Moon

2 . A phone

3 . an igloo

Types of articles

Definite - THE

Indefinite - A/AN

Definite article - The

"The" is called the definite article . It defines the noun as

1 . Something specific

2 . Something previouly mentioned or known

3 something unique

A

We use "a" before the nouns that begin with a consonant sound .

It is used for singular noun.

AN

We use "an" before the nouns that begin with a vowel sound .

It is also used with singular noun.

Exercise

Q1 . Fill with article .

1 . My uncle is ______ eye specialist .

2 . Ajay is _____ best player in our football team .

3 . Nile is ____ longest river of world .

4 . I need ____ kilogram of sugar .

5 . It takes ____ hour to get there.

6 . I saw ____ old mam in _________ new year party ..

CHAPTER FOUR

Tenses

Get set go ...

2 Tenses areform of verb that shows when an action happened .

Types of tenses

Simple present tense

It describes everday actions .

for ex-

I eat bread and butter for breakfast .

I always study after coming from school .

present continuous tense

It tells what is happening now .

For ex

1 . Frank is washing the dishes .

2 . Anandi is driving the car .

Simple past tense

Tells what has already happened

For ex-

1 . Niharika slipped down the stairs .
2 . She sang a lovely song.

Simple future tense

Tells what is yet to happened

For ex-
1 . I will see you tomorrow .
2 . Kate will submit the books to library .
exercise
Q1 . Write the type of tense in each sentence .
1 . I will bring the book tomorrow .
2 . The Earth revolves around the Sun .
3 . She slept .
Q2 . Change them to past continuous tense .
1 . Naina is doing a jigsaw puzzle .
ans -
2 . They are sleeping .
ans -
3 . The children are sleeping .
ans -

Past continuous tense

It is used when we talk about things that were happening at a particular place .

We use was and were in this .
For ex-
1 . Reehan was cleaning the house .
2 . I was sleeping when guests arrived .
Compre

CHAPTER FIVE

Preposition

A preposition is a word or group of words used before a noun, pronoun, or noun phrase to show direction, time, place, location, spatial relationships, or to introduce an object. Some examples of prepositions are words like "in," "at," "on," "of," and "to." Prepositions in English are highly idiomatic.

Some examples of common prepositions used in sentences are:

He sat on the chair.

There is some milk in the fridge.

She was hiding under the table.

The cat jumped off the counter.

He drove over the bridge.

She lost her ring at the beach.

The book belongs to Anthony.

They were sitting by the tree.

Preposition of Place

What is a preposition of place?

A preposition of place is a preposition which is used to refer to a place where something or someone is located. There are only three prepositions of place, however they can be used to discuss an almost endless number of places.

At – A preposition of place which is used to discuss a certain point

In – A preposition of place which is used to discuss an enclosed space

On – A preposition of time which is used to discuss a surface

Examples of Prepositions of Place

Prepositions of place give you the ability to tell others where something is located. In the following examples, the prepositions of place have been italicized for ease of identification.

Jessie waited for Jim at the corner.

The mall is located at the intersection of Main Street and Third Avenue.

We spent a quiet evening at home.

I'm growing tomatoes in my garden.

Marie was born in Paris, France.

I was so tired that I took a nap in the car.

Please place the bouquet on the table.

I really wish you would stop throwing your dirty clothes on the floor.

What's on the menu this evening?

Preposition of movement

Prepositions of Movement! A preposition can provide us with information on the relationship between two words within a sentence, one such relationship is movement of something in the sentence. For example, 'the car drove along the street' This shows us where something was going and allows us to understand what is being talked about more clearly.

In this section, we are going to show you a detailed list of prepositions of movement which will add to your vocabulary as well as giving yo the ability to create more detailed sentences and sound more fluent.

Preposition of movement examples:

She turned her back to the audience.

He looked straight into her eyes.

She pushed her face towards him.

They rode along narrow country lanes.

Her hair whipped around her face in the wind.

Prepositions of Movement List with Examples

TO

The preposition to is used to indicate a destination or direction.

Examples:

The boys go to school in groups.

Many people travel to work by car.

He got out of bed and walked to the window.

Would you like to run to the harbor to look at the ships?

We're driving to Maryland to look at a drop tank?

He came to England in his infancy.

The preposition to is sometimes used to indicate a specific position, especially if a person or object is facing something.

Examples:

The physics lab is down the hall to your right.

She turned her back to the audience.

TOWARD(S)

The preposition towards is used to say that someone or something moves, looks, faces,... in the direction of someone or something.

Examples:

She pushed her face towards him.

She was carrying a suitcase and walking towards.

THROUGH

The preposition through is used when we talk about movement from one side to another but "in something", such as long grass or a forest.

Examples:

David walked slowly through the woods.

The Charles River flows through Boston.

INTO

The preposition into is used to talk about the movement that enters a space, usually with a verb that expresses movement.

Examples:

Don't put new wine into old bottles.

He looked straight into her eyes.

She swerved and crashed into the fence

OVER

The preposition over refers to movement at a higher level than something else. It also can be used when talking about movement across a surface.

Examples:

He jumped over the wall.

A beautiful white bird flew over the lake.

Over also functions as a preposition expressing position. It often has a similar meaning to the preposition above.

Example:

He lived in a flat above/ over the shop.

ACROSS

The preposition across is used when talking about movement from one side of something to the other which has sides or limits such as a city, road or river. It is also used to when something touches or stretches from one side to another.

Examples:

The boys swam across the lake.

The truck skidded sideways across the road.

It's the first time I've flown across the Atlantic.

ALONG

The preposition along is used to show movement of something in a line that follows the side of something long.

Examples:

We went for a walk along the beach at twilight.

They rode along narrow country lanes.

FROM

The preposition from is used to show the place where someone or something starts.

Example:

What time does the flight from Amsterdam arrive?

AROUND

The preposition around refers to the movement in circles or in the vicinity of something

Example:

Her hair whipped around her face in the wind.

ONTO

The preposition onto is used to talk about movement to a position on a surface, usually with a verb that expresses movement.

Example:

I slipped as I stepped onto the platform.

UP

The preposition up refers to a higher position or movement to a higher position.

Example:

She doesn't like rid

DOWN

The preposition down indicates the movement to a lower position.

Example:

It's easier to run down the hill than go up.

ing her bike up these hills.

EXERCISE

Q1 . Fill in the blanks with suitable preposition of movement .

I don't know how I managed to get ....

I hope you won't run ....

He was trying to throw his hat .... the roof. ...

John always manages to get ....

He threw himself ....

She ran .... the room. ...

I took the envelope ....

Q2 . Fill in the blanks with suitable preposition of place

1 - I always keep some extra money __ my bag in case of emergencies.

in

on

at

2 - I'll read it tonight ___ home.

at

in

on

3 - Do you live ___ a house or an apartment?

on

at

in

4 - Did you learn English ___ Malta?

at

on

in

5 - She grew up ___ a farm.

on

at

in

6 - I read about it ___ the newspaper.

on

in

at

7 - He went for a swim ___ the river

on

in

at

8 - The dog's sleeping ___ the carpet.

at

in

on

9 - The information is ___ the top of the page.

at

on

in

10 - Were you ___ the party too?

in

on

at

Preposition of Time

What is a preposition of time?

A preposition of time is a preposition that allows you to discuss a specific time period such as a date on the calendar, one of the days of the week, or the actual time something takes place. Prepositions of time are the same words as prepositions of place, however they are used in a different way. You can easily distinguish these prepositions, as they always discuss times rather than places.

At – This preposition of time is used to discuss clock times, holidays and festivals, and other very specific time frames including exceptions, such as "at night."

In – This preposition of time is used to discuss months, seasons, years, centuries, general times of day, and longer periods of time such as "in the past."

On – This preposition of time is used to discuss certain days of the week or portions of days of the week, specific dates, and special days such as "on New Year's Day."

Prepositions of time allow you to tell your readers when things are taking place. They are vital parts of speech to use in stories, as well as when writing simple communications, reports, and other items.

Examples of Prepositions of Time

There may only be three prepositions of time, but the ways in which you can use them are almost endless. In the following examples, the prepositions of time have been italicized for ease of identification.

My birthday falls in January.

Birds often migrate in spring and autumn.

EXERCISE

1. I will be here .... next week.

since

for

until

2. The school reopens .... Monday.

on

at

in

3. I invite my friends to dinner .... Christmas eve.

on

in

at

4. They are getting married .... the tenth of August.

in

on

at

5. They will be here from Monday .... Friday.

since

for

to

6. He hasn't worked .... he lost his job.

for

since

until

7. The work won't be complete .... Friday.

since

for

until

8. They are getting married .... the spring.

on

in

at

9. It usually rains .... the month of July.

in

on

at

CHAPTER SIX

Punctuation

Punctuation is the collection of marks that we use to make sentences flow smoothly and express meaning clearly. It tells us when to pause or add a certain feeling to our words; it separates ideas so that sentences are clear, it points out titles, quotes, and other key parts of language—punctuation is important!

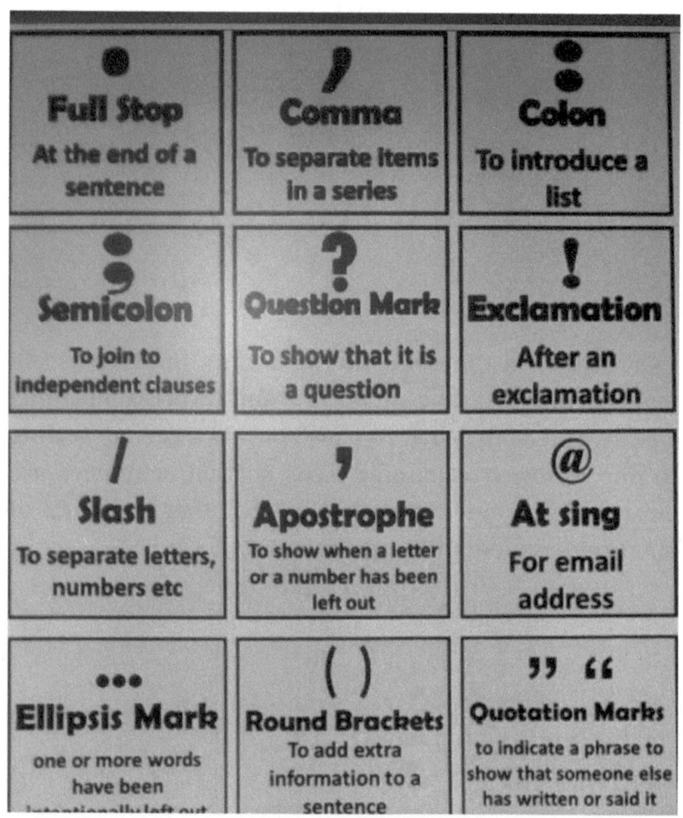

types of punctuation

Comma and Colon

The comma (.), semicolon, and colon can indicate a pause in a series. The comma is used to show a separation of elements within the structure of a sentence.

The semicolon (;) is used to connect two or three independent clauses. It shows a closer relationship between the clauses.

A colon (:) has three main uses. It is used after a word such as introducing a quotation, an explanation, an example.

The second is between independent clauses when the second explains the first, like a semicolon:

I didn't have time to get my passport: I was already late.

A colon is used for emphasis.

Soon again spring will come, trees will bloom.

Apostrophe and Ellipsis

The final punctuation forms in English grammar are the apostrophe, and ellipsis. They are not related to another in any form. An apostrophe (') can be used to indicate the omission of a letter or letters from a word.

Exclamation Mark !

Meaning: Exclamation mark is used immediately after an exclamation.

Example Sentence:

Yes, You will come with me!

Question Mark ?

Meaning: at the end of a phrase or sentence to show that it is a question.

Example Sentence:

How much paper will they need?

At sign @

Meaning: for email address

Ellipsis Mark ...

Meaning: one or more words have been intentionally left out

Example Sentence:

Today ... we started new work.

Quotation Marks " "

Meaning: used to indicate a phrase to show that someone else has written or said it.

Example Sentence:
“I’m very tired.“ she said.
Slash /
Meaning: separate letters, numbers, or words.
Example Sentence:
Free ticket will be given to children/women only.
Square Brackets [ ]
Example Sentence:
It [apple] is really useful fruit.
Underscore _
Example Sentence:
for_you@gmail.com
Dash —
Example Sentence:
I’m very happy.
—me too.
Round Brackets or Parentheses ( )
Example Sentence:
Mary (18 years-old) is a young girl.
Semi colon ;
Example Sentence:
Michael has a big house; Alex has a small house.
Hypen –
Example Sentence:
pick-me-up
Underline _
Example Sentence:
The meeting will be start at 08:00 PM.

CHAPTER SEVEN

Conjunctions

A Conjunction is a word that joins parts of a sentence, phrases or other words together. Conjunctions are used as single words or in pairs. Example: and, but, or are used by themselves, whereas, neither/nor, either/or are conjunction pairs. For Example:

Two **and** eight make ten.

The principal **and** the science teacher were interrogated.

You can remain, **but** I shall go to London.

People study medicine **or** dentistry (nouns) when they enroll at that institution.

The spectators had juice **and** cookies (nouns).

That restaurant is known for healthy **and** nutritious (adjectives) food.

I'm buying either the striped **or** paisley (adjectives) wallpaper.

He continued arguing **until** everyone finally agreed with him.

They came out to play football **when** the rain started falling.

John will renew his renew his rent **once** he gets his salary.

She listened to him politely, **even though** his comments sounded silly.

They couldn't get into the house **since** they misplaced the keys.

If he knew the truth, her father would throw the doll away.

When I brought my first paycheck home, I wanted to frame it.

Once he gets his salary, John will renew his rent.

Since they misplaced the keys, they couldn't get into the house.

When, after, before, until, since, while, once, as and as soon as are subordinating conjunctions which can be used to connect an action or an event to a point in time.

action/event

conjunction

time

She was in a bad car accident

when

she was young.

We can't play loud music

after

everyone has gone to bed.

When, after, before, until, since, while, once, as and as soon as are subordinating conjunctions which can be used to connect an action or an event to a point in time.

action/event

conjunction

time

She was in a bad car accident

when

she was young.

We can't play loud music

after

everyone has gone to bed.

Sample paper 1 CH 1 TO 7

Q1 . underline subject .

The sun was shining brightly.

The dogs were barking loudly.

The pretty girl was wearing a blue frock.

My younger brother serves in the army.

The man and his wife were working in their garden.

My mother and my aunt are trained classical dancers.

You don't have to wait for me.

We will no longer tolerate this.

The little tree was covered with needles instead of leaves.

A rich merchant was passing by the shoemaker's window.

Q2 . Underline predicate

The sun was shining brightly.

The dogs were barking loudly.

The pretty girl was wearing a blue frock.

My younger brother serves in the army.

The man and his wife were working in their garden.

My mother and my aunt are trained classical dancers.

You don't have to wait for me.

We will no longer tolerate this.

The little tree was covered with needles instead of leaves.

A rich merchant was passing by the shoemaker's window.

Fill correct article

.... man is mortal. ...

I am .... university student. ...

She goes to the temple in .... mornings. ...

Kiran is .... best student in the class. ...

.... camel is the ship of the desert. ...

This book has won .... Booker prize. ...

Harishchandra was .... honest king. ...

I am fond of ....

Fill blank with simple present tense .

1. I ————— at a bank.

work

works

working

2. She ——————– with her parents.

live

lives

living

3. Cows ———————– on grass.

feed

feeds

feeding

4. He ———————- a handsome salary.

earn

earns

earning

5. Janet ———————- to be a singer.

want

wants

wanting

6. Emily ——————- delicious cookies.

make

makes

making

7. Arti and her husband —————- in Singapore.

live

lives

living

8. Rohan and Sania ——————- to play card games.

like

likes

liking

9. Sophia ——————— English very well.

speak

speaks

speaking

10. Martin ——————– for a walk in the morning.

go

goes

going

11. My grandfather —————– his pet dog.

adore

adores

adoring

12. Plants ——————– water and sunlight for making their food.

need

needs

needing

Fill blank with present continuous tense .

I ___________a horse. (ride)

You __________ with us right now. (come)

She _________ on the floor. (not/dance)

Yes, Ram is _______ today's event. (host)

The Chief Minister is _______ the flag. (hoist)

____ they _______ in the drama? (act)

He is ______ his new business. (start)

She _______ them the value of education. (realize)

Am I ________ you right now? (trouble)

He is _______ the workshop. (open)

She is ________ her limits. (cross)

____ they ______ from the top of the mountain? (jump)

He is _______ everyone who come in front of him.(not/ kill)

You are ________ us for the trip. (join)

The teacher ________ all the students from his lecture. (annoy)

Fill blank with simple past tense.

1) They all (go) ___ shopping.

2) I never (imagine) ____ I would see you here.

3) We (book) ___ two tickets for the show.

4) He (collect) ___ his children from school.

5) Were you (frighten) ___ of the dark when you were young?

6) Who (eat) ___ my chocolate?

7) I (feel) so tired that I went straight to bed.

8) We (grow) ___ this tree from a seed.

9) She (lose) ___ her way home.

Fill blank with simple future tense.

1. In two days, I .... my results.

will know

would know

will be knowing

2. ‘There is the doorbell.’ ‘I ....’

would go

am going

will go

3. You .... this decision.

will be regretting

will regret

would regret

4. We .... what happened to her.

would never know

will never know

will never be knowing

5. The whole nation .... proud of you.

is

will be

would be

6. That .... our gift to the school.

will be

would be

will have been

7. Kind words .... others joy.

will give

would give

will be giving

8. This piece of wisdom .... you ten dollars.

will cost

would cost

will be costing

9. You .... my position.

will never understand

would never understand

never understand

10. Someday I .... a novel.

will be writing

will write

would write

11. I .... this.

will not permit

would not permit

will not be permitting

12. He .... the test.

cannot pass

will not pass

will not be passing

Fill blank with past continuous tense

1. My brother and sister _____ playing tennis at 11AM yesterday.

are

was

were

2. _____ you still working at 7PM last night?

Were

Are

Was

3. At 8.30AM today I _____ driving to work.

was

am

were

4. We _____ sleeping when the police came.

was

weren't

won't

5. Why _____ he having lunch at 4PM?

was
does
were

6. Was he not _____ his homework?

doing
do
done

7. Snow _____ lightly. Suddenly a reindeer appeared.

fell
was falling
is falling

8. Somebody threw a shoe at him _____ he was speaking.

after
when
while

9. They ________ TV when I arrived.

were watching
were watched
watched

10. I was reading a detective story _____ I heard a noise.

during
while
when

Fill blank with correct preposition.

1. We walked .... the edge of the desert.

Please select 2 correct answers

as far as

up to

until

2. It is another three weeks .... the holidays.

Please select 2 correct answers

to

until

for

up to

3. I don't know how she manages to support such a large family. She has nothing .... her pension.

besides

except

apart from

All of the above

4. Are you wearing anything .... your sweater?

below

under

underneath

Either under or underneath

5. Do you mind? I was .... you!

Please select 2 correct answers

in front of

in front off

before

6. We should arrive .... their place .... time .... lunch.

at, in, for

in, to, at

at, for, in

at, by, for

7. They live .... a small one bedroom flat .... the third floor.

in, in

on, on

in, on

on, in

8. Granny is arriving .... the 3.30 train.

in

with

on

9. Last year, there were a large number of mangoes .... the tree.

in

at

on

with

10. His house is .... the way from Mumbai to Thane.

in

at

by

on

11. He met and fell in love with a French girl when he was .... the London School of Economics.

in

at

on

12. A few days after the accident she died .... the injuries.

of

with

from

Use appropriate punctuation marks in the following sentences.

1. We had a great time in France the kids really enjoyed it
2. Some people work best in the mornings others do

better in the evenings

3. What are you doing next weekend

4. Mother had to go into hospital she had heart problems

5. Did you understand why I was upset

6. It is a fine idea let us hope that it is going to work

7. We will be arriving on Monday morning at least I think so

8. A textbook can be a wall between teacher and class

9. The girls father sat in a corner

10. In the words of Murphys Law Anything that can go wrong will go wrong

Complete the following sentences with an appropriate conjunction.

1. John smokes .... his brother doesn't.

but

and

so

2. Neither Alice .... Mary has come.

or

nor

3. She speaks English .... Spanish.

Please select 2 correct answers

as well as

and

Either could be used here

4. I like him .... he is very sincere.

so

because

hence

5. .... he worked hard, he did not win.

Though

As if

As though

6. She is ill .... she is cheerful.

and

but

as well as

7. .... it was raining we decided to go out.

Despite

Though

However

8. The piper played .... the children danced.

or

and

but

Complete the following sentences with an appropriate conjunction.

1. John smokes .... his brother doesn't.

but

and

so

2. Neither Alice .... Mary has come.

or

nor

3. She speaks English .... Spanish.

Please select 2 correct answers

as well as

and

Either could be used here

4. I like him .... he is very sincere.

so

because

hence

5. .... he worked hard, he did not win.

Though

As if

As though

6. She is ill .... she is cheerful.

and

but

as well as

7. .... it was raining we decided to go out.

Despite

Though

However

8. The piper played .... the children danced.

or

and

but

9. James works hard .... his brother is lazy.

as

as long as

whereas

10. I went to the shop .... bought some vegetables.

and

so

hence

11. You must start at once; .... you will be late.

whereas

otherwise

as long as

12. He must be tired .... he has been working since morning.

so

hence

because

Writing essay

Title of essay

Introduction - What are the names of three activities you like ? Describe each activity briefly .

Body(100) words - Who encourages you to do those activities?Which activity do you like the most and why ?

Conclusion(50) words - Do you think any of these activities would hold your interest for long ?

CHAPTER EIGHT

Interjection

An interjection is a kind of exclamation inserted into regular speech. Actually, it is a brief and abrupt pause in speech for expressing emotions. They are unique and have some interesting features: Interjections don't have a grammatical function in sentence construction.

for ex

Wow! Lisa is looking gorgeous.

Hurray! Our team has won the match.

Hey! Are you serious?

Alas! John's father died yesterday.

Yippee! We are going on vacation.

Hi! Where have you been?

Oh! The place is so crowded.

What! You have broken the glass of the window.

rules for interjection

i) If the interjection forms a sentence alone, follow it with a full stop, question or exclamation mark. ii) If the interjection comes at the

EXERCISE

Question 1:

Identify the interjection and underline it.

Hmm, I'm not sure this colour is perfect for my dress.

Uh oh! The police has caught him.

I guess that's the end of the series, darn.

Hello! How do you do?

Of course! I'll make all the arrangements for your birthday.

Ouch! It's paining badly.

Alas! She's dead now.

Oh, it's been around a month since I saw him.

Q2 . Choose the Right Interjection

Directions: In the following sentences, choose the most appropriate interjection from the selection below and write it in the space provided.

Choose from: Wow, Seriously, Goodness, Dang, Yippee, Incredible, Bingo, Geez, Yay, Darn

_______________, why didn't you hold the door for me?

_______________, I'm so happy that you decided to visit this summer.

_______________, it's not every day that you see a dog riding a skateboard.

_______________! How can you possibly agree with that point of view?

He just cost us the game with that error, _______________!

_______________! You just gave me a great idea.

_______________, that's a very large dog at the end of that leash.

I can't believe that I finally got an A on a project, _____________!

_______________, my favorite author is doing a reading at the local library.

This is my first new car,________________.

9 798886 298260

Printed by Libri Plureos GmbH in Hamburg,
Germany